FANTASTIC FACTS ABOUT

SPACE EXPLORATION

Author
Tim Furniss

Editor
Steve Parker

Design
Pentacor

Image Coordination
Ian Paulyn

Production Assistant
Rachel Jones

Index
Jane Parker

Editorial Director
Paula Borton

Design Director
Clare Sleven

Publishing Director
Jim Miles

This is a Parragon Publishing Book

This edition is published in 2001

Parragon Publishing, Queen Street House, 4 Queen Street, Bath BA1 1HE, UK

Copyright Parragon © 2000

Parragon has previously printed this material in 1999 as part of the Factfinder series

2 4 6 8 10 9 7 5 3 1

Produced by Miles Kelly Publishing Ltd
Bardfield Centre, Great Bardfield, Essex CM7 4SL

ISBN 0-75255-605-3

Printed in China

FANTASTIC FACTS ABOUT

SPACE EXPLORATION

p

CONTENTS

Introduction 6

SPACE EXPLORATION 8
Lifting Off 10
Exploring the Sun 12
Visiting Mercury 14
Venus Unveiled 16
The Earth from Space 18
Probes to the Moon 20
Mission to Mars 22
Flying Past Jupiter 24
Into the Unknown 26
Visitors to Saturn 28
The World of Uranus 30
Journey to Neptune 32
Beyond Our System 34

ROCKETS AND SATELLITES 36
Early Rockets 38

Launchers 40
Satellite Technology 42
Navigation Satellites 44

SPACE PROGRAMS 46
Race to the Moon 48
First Apollo Flights 50
Man on the Moon 52

SHUTTLES AND STATIONS 54
The Space Shuttle 56
Sky Lab 58
The Mir Space Station 60

Index 62
Acknowledgments 64

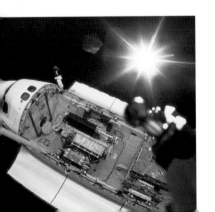

INTRODUCTION

For hundreds of years the only way of exploring space was by using a telescope. Today, with the astonishing advances of science and technology, spacecraft have explored almost every planet in our solar system, and humans have walked on the Moon. Find out about the rockets, stations, probes, and other objects we send into space, rapidly increasing our knowledge about the Universe as we begin the 21st century.

SPACE EXPLORATION is a handy reference guide in the *Fascinating Facts* series. Each book has been specially compiled with a collection of stunning illustrations and photographs which bring the subject to life. Hundreds of facts and figures are presented in a variety of interesting ways and fact-panels provide information at-a-glance. This unique combination is fun and easy to use and makes learning a pleasure.

SPACE EXPLORATION

Spacecrafts have now visited every planet in our Solar System, except the most distant planet, Pluto. Our exploration of space began when the first artificial satellite, *Sputnik 1*, circled the Earth in 1957. Within a few years, both the United States and the Soviet Union were sending rockets to the Moon to prepare the way for the first astronauts to land on its surface. Spacecrafts have been sent to explore the planets, some flying past their target or orbiting around it, while

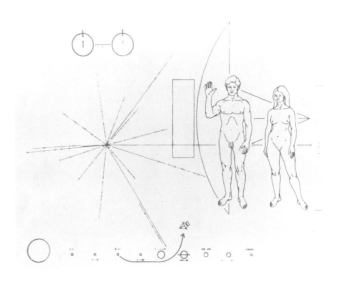

others land on the planet's surface. These spacecrafts send back valuable images and other data, allowing scientists to build up increasingly detailed information about our family of planets. Spacecrafts have investigated other objects in space too, including comets and the band of asteroids between Jupiter and Mars.

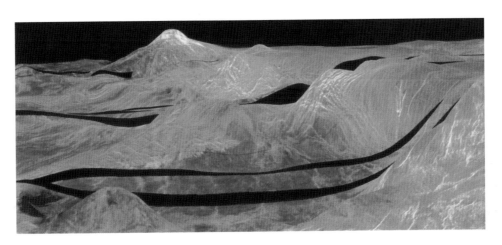

LIFTING OFF

For hundreds of years the only way to explore the planets was by using telescopes. All this changed in December 1962, when the American spacecraft *Mariner 2* flew past Venus. It sent back the first data about the planet, indicating that it was an extremely hot place. Since then, spacecrafts have explored every planet in our Solar System, except Pluto, and have also visited a comet and some asteroids.

Craft have landed on Venus and Mars, and have penetrated the swirling atmosphere of Jupiter. Other spacecrafts have orbited Venus, Mars, and Jupiter, while several planets have received fleeting visits from passing spacecrafts. Closer to the Earth, the first rocket was launched to the Moon in 1958, and since then 12 men have walked on the Earth's nearest neighbor. Spacecrafts have also explored the Sun closely. Through space technology our knowledge of the Solar System has reached new and very exciting limits.

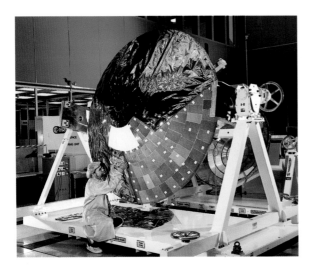

A VISITOR TO SATURN
The US/European Cassini–Huygens *spacecraft took 10 years to build. It is now on its way for a rendezvous with the planet Saturn in July 2004.* Cassini *will orbit Saturn while the* Huygens *probe will land on its moon, Titan.*

FIRST LANDING ON MARS
A Titan III-E Centaur D1
booster rocket launched the Viking 1
spacecraft on August 20, 1975. The
NASA spacecraft made the first soft
landing on Mars.

ANOTHER WORLD

The *Huygens* probe is
expected to reveal Titan's
surface as a world of methane
seas, methane icebergs,
methane snow, and a mixture
of ice and rock. It will be
dark, because the sunlight that
filters through the orangy
clouds gives a similar light
to the light provided on
Earth by a Full Moon.
The main gas in Titan's
atmosphere is nitrogen, and
some scientists think that the
orangy clouds may contain
some organic material. This
material is similar to that
which has been created by
scientists who are trying to
simulate the formation of
life on Earth.

LANDING ON TITAN
The European Space Agency's
probe Huygens *should touch*
down on Saturn's moon,
Titan, in November 2004.
If this happens, it will be the
first landing on the moon of
a planet other than the Earth.

EXPLORING THE SUN

The Sun has come under detailed scrutiny by a whole fleet of spacecraft since 1959, when the *Pioneer 4* spacecraft entered solar orbit after missing the Moon. Scientists were particularly interested in the particles of solar energy which affect the Earth and its upper atmosphere. They also wanted to try and understand how the Sun actually works. In 1962, the United States launched missions of Earth-orbiting solar observatories, called OSO. Later, two Helios spacecrafts and several other Pioneer spacecrafts were sent to operate in orbit around the Sun.

Special instruments on board the space station *Skylab* in 1973 and 1974 took images of the Sun in different wavelengths.

They revealed activity within the Sun's atmosphere that cannot be seen in visible light. *Skylab* carried its own solar telescope mounted on the outside of the station. More recently, the European Solar and Heliospheric Observatory (SOHO) was launched to conduct non-stop observations of the Sun, rather like a solar weather station.

*SOHO OBSERVATORY
The European Solar and Heliospheric Observatory (SOHO) was launched in 1995. It will conduct the most comprehensive observation so far of the Sun and its radiation.*

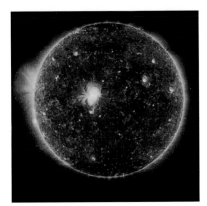

3.6 million degrees
Fahrenheit
(2 million degrees Celsius)

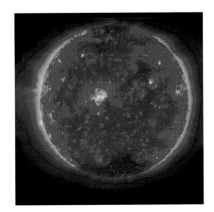

2.7 degrees million
Fahrenheit
(1.5 million degrees Celsius)

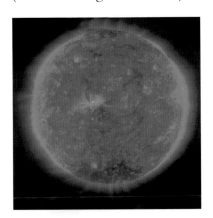

1.8 million degrees
Fahrenheit
(1 million degrees Celsius)

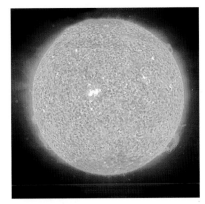

144,000 degrees
Fahrenheit
(80,000 degrees Celsius)

SURVEYING THE SUN

SOHO was placed into a special orbit 900 million miles (1.5 billion km) from the Earth. This orbit gives SOHO an uninterrupted view of the Sun from a point in space where the forces of gravity from the Sun and the Earth are equal. SOHO is part of an international program involving satellites from many countries. Their intensive survey of the Sun and its effect on the Earth is called the Solar Terrestrial Science Program.

IMAGES FROM SOHO
These ultraviolet images from SOHO show the different temperatures in the Sun's atmosphere. SOHO studied the Sun's surface activity, atmosphere, and radiation, including the solar wind. The study was made from a unique orbit that provided an uninterrupted view of the Sun.

VISITING MERCURY

 It is almost impossible to view Mercury's surface with a telescope. In fact, until 1973 almost the only thing we knew about the closest planet to the Sun was that it must be very hot! The first, and so far the only, spacecraft to visit Mercury is *Mariner 10,* which was launched on November 3, 1973. Its flight path took it to Mercury using a fly-by of Venus. The spacecraft used the gravitational force of Venus as a "sling shot" to divert it onto the right course.

Mariner 10 made three separate fly-bys of Mercury, coming to within 3,576 miles (5,768 km) of the planet on March 29, 1974, within 436 miles (703 km) on September 21, 1974, and within 29,803 miles (48,069 km) on March 16, 1975. The images from the spacecraft were astonishing. Mercury is just like the Moon! It has thousands of craters, including a huge meteorite crater called the Caloris Basin.

VIEW FROM MARINER 10
Mariner 10 *gave us the first and only clear view of Mercury, showing it to be surprisingly like our Moon.*

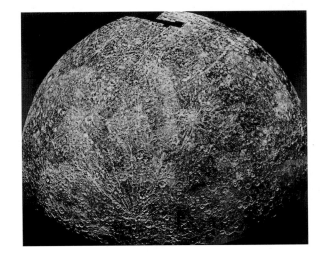

MARINER 10 MISSION

Mariner 10 was a cut-price spacecraft flying a cut-price mission! To save money it was launched by a less powerful booster rocket, and as a result it needed to use Venus as a "sling shot". This meant that *Mariner 10* had to pass within a 240–mile (400–km) target area about 3,000 miles (5,000 km) from Venus, or else it would miss the opportunity to visit Mercury. To do this, the spacecraft had to fire its own engine very accurately several times during its journey.

FLYING PAST MERCURY

Mariner 10 *was launched in 1975. It was the first spacecraft to be sent to explore two planets in a single mission. It flew past Venus once and past Mercury three times.*

VENUS UNVEILED

Venus is a hostile planet and has posed a great challenge to space engineers. They have nonetheless succeeded in mapping almost the whole planet and have even landed crafts on its surface. Venus is surrounded by thick clouds of carbon dioxide gas that create a surface temperature of about 830 degrees Fahrenheit (460 degrees C).

The planet has an atmospheric pressure 90 times that of the Earth. It was first explored successfully by *Mariner 2* in 1962. The Soviet craft *Venera 4* penetrated the clouds, sending back some data in 1967, and in 1970 *Venera 7*'s capsule reached the surface still intact. *Veneras 9* and *10* became the first Venus orbiters in 1975, and their landing capsules sent

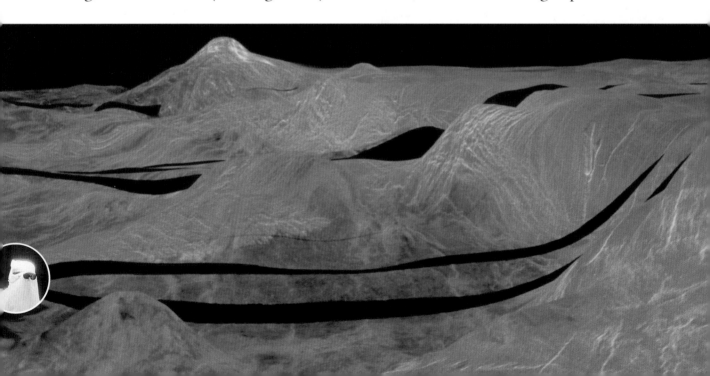

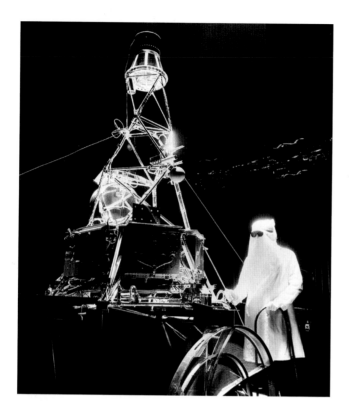

FLYING PAST VENUS

The first successful explorer of our Solar System was the 446-pound (203-kg) Mariner 2 spacecraft. It flew past Venus at a distance of 21,080 miles (34,000 km) on December 14, 1962.

back the first pictures of the surface — an extraordinary feat in view of the harsh conditions. Further Venera probes included those that sent back some radar images that penetrated the thick cloud. More recently, the *Magellan* Venus orbiter was deployed from the space shuttle in 1989.

IMAGES FROM MAGELLAN

The Magellan *radar mapping satellite generated false-color images of what the surface of Venus looked like beneath the thick clouds.*

LANDING ON VENUS

The earlier Venera probes proved that these spacecrafts did not need parachutes to complete their landing on Venus's surface because its atmosphere is so dense. *Veneras 9* and *10* landed at a speed of 26 feet per second. They were protected by an ingenious shock-absorbing system, rather like a lifebelt. The capsule sat in the center of a ring that was inflated with gas before the landing. An airbraking disk on top of the capsule also served as the radio transmitter.

THE EARTH FROM SPACE

 The first astronauts to travel to the Moon were also the first to see the Earth as it might appear to explorers from another planet. On seeing the Earth as a tiny part of an enormous Universe, the *Apollo 8* astronaut James Lovell described our planet as a "grand oasis in the vastness of space". The *Apollo 8* crew's famous picture of the Earth as seen from space seemed to sum up Lovell's feelings.

After traveling into space to explore the Moon, the Apollo crew came back with something much more precious for the world's population — an appreciation of our tiny Earth as a fragile planet. As a result, there was an enormous increase in people's concern for the Earth's environment. People were also struck by the lack of real boundaries on the Earth's surface, unlike the view of the Earth that we see in a geography atlas.

THE RISING EARTH
In this picture taken during the Apollo 11 *mission the Earth seems to be rising above the surface of the Moon. The astronauts actually saw the Earth coming into sight around the side of the Moon.*

OUR BEAUTIFUL EARTH

For any astronaut, a view of the Earth from space is a captivating sight. Photos can never fully reveal the Earth's beauty and color.

VIEW OF THE WORLD

This classic view of the Earth was taken by the Apollo 17 *crew on their way to the Moon in December 1972. It clearly shows the land masses of Africa and Saudi Arabia, with the continent of Antarctica below.*

19

PROBES TO THE MOON

 Soon after the first satellites were launched into orbit above the Earth, the next obvious target in space was the Moon. The first attempts to send probes to the Moon were made in 1958, but the first object to hit the Moon's surface was the Soviet *Luna 2* spacecraft in September 1959. Later, *Luna 3* flew round the far side of the Moon, revealing what it looked like for the first time. Ranger probes took close-up photos before they crashed onto the surface in 1964 and 1965.

The first soft landings on the Moon were made by Luna and Surveyor craft in 1966. The unmanned *Luna 16* brought back samples from the Moon in 1970, the year in which the Soviet Union also launched an unmanned lunar rover called Lunakhod. After the first astronauts landed on the Moon in 1969, unmanned flights became rarer. *Luna 24* made the final flight of this era in 1976.

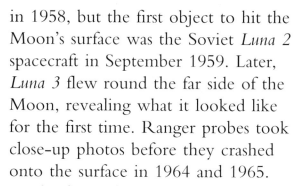

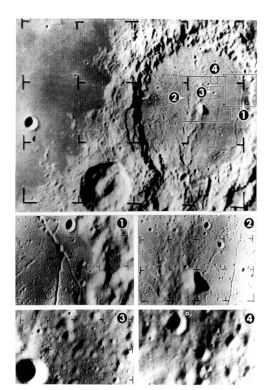

DESCENT TO THE MOON
These photos were taken on March 24, 1965 by the US spacecraft Ranger 9. *It was plunging toward the inside of the Alphonsus crater on the near side of the Moon.*

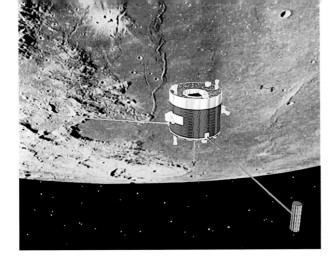

LUNAR PROSPECTOR
Launched in January 1998, Lunar Prospector *carried out a detailed chemical analysis of the Moon. The results confirmed that there might be frozen water under the bedrock in the polar regions.*

WATER ON THE MOON

New interest in unmanned exploration of the Moon began when the US spacecraft *Clementine* was launched in 1994. It sent back data indicating that there may be frozen water under the rock around the Moon's poles. In 1998, NASA's *Lunar Prospector* began orbiting the poles and seemed to confirm this information. The water exists as ice crystals in the soil. If Moon bases are built at some time in the future, a water-extraction plant on the Moon would be needed to make use of this resource.

SURVEYING THE MOON
The US Surveyor spacecraft made the first rocket-assisted touchdowns on the lunar surface in 1966 and 1967. Some of the Surveyor craft carried robot arms fitted with scoops to collect soil samples.

MISSIONS TO MARS

Mars has always held a particular fascination for the human mind because it is linked with the possibility that life may have existed on the planet at some time. The first Mars probe was launched in November 1960 but failed. This Soviet attempt was followed by many more, which, apart from *Mars 5* in 1974, all failed. In contrast to the failure of the Soviet missions to Mars, American spacecrafts to the planet met with spectacular successes. The first was *Mariner 4,* which took the first close-up images in 1965. *Mariner 9* went into orbit around Mars in 1971, and two Viking landers scooped up soil and took pictures in 1976.

In 1997 the *Pathfinder* spacecraft captured the world's imagination when it landed its *Sojourner* rover vehicle on the surface of Mars. The main quest now is to bring samples of Martian soil back to Earth. This task may be achieved by about 2007, after a series of lander–rover–orbiter and ascent vehicle missions that are due to start in 2003.

VIKING SPACECRAFT ON MARS
The first soft landings on the planet Mars were made by the American Viking 1 *and* 2 *spacecraft. They sent back the first photos of the Martian surface in 1976.*

IS THERE WATER ON MARS?

The Mars Climate Orbiter will enter polar orbit around Mars in September 1999. It will also act as a data relay satellite for the Mars Polar Lander, which is due to land on the edge of the largely frozen carbon dioxide polar cap about 600 miles (1,000 km) from the planet's south pole. A robotic arm will scoop up soil and deliver it to an on-board analyser. Scientists hope to find some evidence of the water that probably flowed across the Martian surface many years ago.

PATHFINDER TO MARS
After the Viking missions of 1976, the next soft landing on Mars was made 21 years later by the Pathfinder *spacecraft (far left). It carried a tiny roving vehicle called* Sojourner *(near left).*

LATEST VISITORS TO MARS
The next assault on the Red Planet got under way in December 1998 with the launch of the Mars Climate Orbiter *(top). This was followed by the* Mars Polar Lander *(bottom), which was launched in January 1999.*

FLYING PAST JUPITER

Four spacecrafts have explored Jupiter, the giant planet of the Solar System. The first was *Pioneer 10,* which was launched in March 1972 and flew past Jupiter at a distance of 80,600 miles (130,000 km) on December 5, 1973. One of its most spectacular images was a close-up of the Great Red Spot. *Pioneer 11* followed on December 3, 1974 at a closer distance of 26,000 miles (42,000 km). It used Jupiter's gravity to sling it onto a course to make a rendezvous with the planet Saturn. The next visitor to Jupiter was *Voyager 1,* which was launched in September 1997 and flew past the planet at a distance of 173,600 miles (280,000 km) on March 5, 1979. It was followed closely by *Voyager 2*, which was launched first but arrived on July 9, 1979, at the closest-ever distance of 400,000 miles (645,000 km). Jupiter's most recent visitor is the *Galileo* spacecraft.

IMAGES FROM VOYAGER
Two Voyager spacecrafts flew past Jupiter in 1979. They returned spectacular pictures of the giant planet and its many moons.

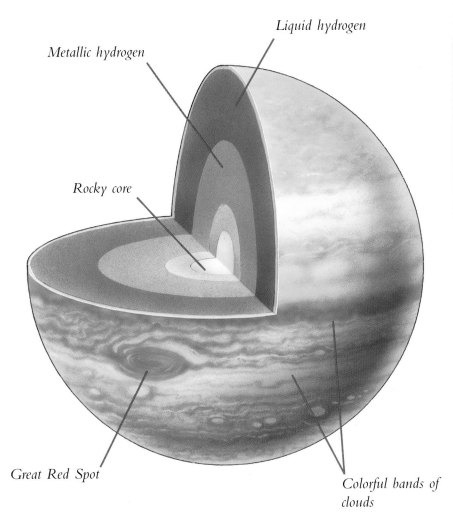

Metallic hydrogen

Liquid hydrogen

Rocky core

Great Red Spot

Colorful bands of clouds

Most of Jupiter is made up of gases, mainly hydrogen and helium. The swirling clouds are divided into a series of bands of different colors, mostly white, brown, and orange. Inside the clouds are crystals of frozen ammonia and frozen water, and molecules of carbon, sulfur and phosphorus. Below the cloud level is a huge sea of liquid hydrogen, and then a layer of metallic hydrogen. Here the pressure on the hydrogen is so great that it starts to behave like a liquid metal. Electricity flows through the metallic hydrogen and creates a strong magnetic field around the planet. At the center of Jupiter is a solid core of rocky material — it is about 20 times more massive than the Earth.

BEYOND THE CLOUDS
Thick clouds swirl around Jupiter, hiding the planet's surface from view. The different bands of color in the clouds are known as belts (the dark bands) and zones (the light-colored areas between belts).

25

INTO THE UNKNOWN

 The space probe *Galileo* was deployed from the space shuttle in October 1989. It became the first Jupiter orbiter in December 1995. The probe entered Jupiter's atmosphere of thick cloud, plunging into the swirling unknown at a speed of 30 miles (47 km) per second. *Galileo* sent back data for a total of 57 minutes, reaching a distance of 98 miles (157 km) inside the clouds. It was finally defeated by very high temperatures and by an atmospheric pressure 22 times higher than the Earth's. Scientists were disappointed with the data from the probe. There seems to be just one layer of cloud, with wind speeds of 2,110 feet (643 m) per second caused by Jupiter's internal heat.

AN EXCITING MOON
One of the most exciting moons orbiting Jupiter is Europa. It may consist of an ocean of liquid water beneath a thin ice cap marked with thousands of cracks hundreds of miles long.

26

INTO JUPITER'S ATMOSPHERE
The first, and so far the only, craft to enter Jupiter's atmosphere is the Galileo *capsule. It plunged into the tops of the planet's dense clouds on December 7, 1995.*

THE GREAT RED SPOT

Jupiter's Great Red Spot was first noticed by an English astronomer, Robert Hooke, in 1664. The oval-shaped spot is 31,000 miles (50,000 km) long and about one-third as wide. It is big enough to swallow up four whole Earths. The Great Red Spot varies in intensity and color. For example, it has recently been measured as only 24,000 miles (40,000 km) long. It is a huge whirlpool of storm winds situated in the planet's southern hemisphere. The red color indicates that it contains a lot of phosphorus, which has been carried upward from the planet's interior. The Great Red Spot slowly changes its position from one year to the next. It can be observed through an ordinary telescope.

VISITORS TO SATURN

 The first spacecraft to visit Saturn was *Pioneer 11*, which flew on to the ringed planet after its rendezvous with Jupiter. It passed the planet at a distance of 13,000 miles (21,000 km) on September 1, 1979. The first discovery it made was that Saturn's ring system does not consist of four divisions as seen in telescopes but of thousands of individual ringlets. Next, *Voyager 1,* which arrived on November 12, 1980 passing at a distance of 76,900 miles (124,000 km), followed by *Voyager 2* passing by at 62,600 miles (101,000 km) on 26 August 1981. The images returned from these crafts revealed Saturn's spectacular ring system in all its glory, as well as many of the planet's

CASSINI ORBITER
NASA's Cassini
spacecraft will deliver
the Huygens *probe*
into the atmosphere of
Titan. It will then
orbit Saturn and relay
data from the
probe back to
Earth.

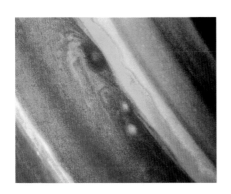

SATURN'S CLOUD

The dense layer of clouds that covers Saturn rotates around the planet every 10 hours. Under the clouds are thick lakes of liquid hydrogen surrounding an inner core of rocky material.

moons in great detail and its cloud bands. The next visitor to Saturn will arrive in 2004, when the US orbiter *Cassini* will become the first spacecraft to orbit the planet. It will send the European *Huygens* probe to land on the

RINGS AND RINGLETS

The Voyager spacecraft confirmed that Saturn has a seventh ring. The probes found that the planet's seven rings are really thousands of separate ringlets. Each ringlet consists of billions of objects ranging in size from icebergs 33 feet wide to tiny specks of ice smaller than a pinhead. The three small moons found in Saturn's ring system were named Prometheus, Pandora, and Atlas. They help to keep all the parts of the rings in place by means of small gravitational forces. These small moons were nicknamed the "shepherd" moons.

LANDING ON TITAN

The Cassini *spacecraft will carry the* Huygens *piggyback probe. The probe will parachute down onto the surface of Titan, Saturn's largest moon. Titan is one of the few moons in the Solar System to have an atmosphere.*

THE WORLD OF URANUS

 Voyager 2 arrived for a close encounter with Uranus on January 24, 1986, at a distance of 44,000 miles (71,000 km). Until then, very little was known about the planet or its newly discovered ring system. The visit by the Voyager spacecraft changed all that. It found 10 new moons, all of them inside the orbits of the five known satellites. Two new rings were discovered, and two of the new moons seemed to be acting as "shepherds", rather like those discovered in the rings of Saturn.

Little was revealed of the planet itself beneath its greenish-blue atmosphere of hydrogen and helium. Because *Voyager 2* was being targeted

RINGS AROUND URANUS
This combined image was taken by the remarkable Voyager 2 *spacecraft. It shows part of the moon, Miranda, as well as the planet's ring system and Uranus itself.*

at another destination, Neptune, the craft's close flight path across Uranus lasted only about 5 hours. Signals from *Voyager 2*, which was 1.79 billion miles (2.88 billion km) away, took 2 hours 25 minutes to reach the Earth.

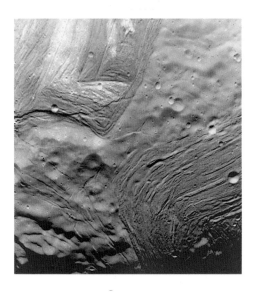

MIRANDA

Miranda is the smallest moon of Uranus. Its amazing surface is covered with a huge variety of features, including faults, grooves, terraces, and a steep cliff 10 miles (16 km) high.

FIVE MOONS

Voyager 2 made close-up images of the five known moons of Uranus: the cratered Oberon, bright Ariel, frosty Titania, dark Ombriel, and the amazing Miranda. Geologists have suggested that Miranda had fragmented at least a dozen times and re-formed in its present jumbled state, like a jigsaw puzzle put together in the wrong way. This theory may be linked to the fact that the rings of Uranus were found to consist of boulders rather than small particles. One of the ten new moons discovered, called Puck, was only 106 miles (170 km) across.

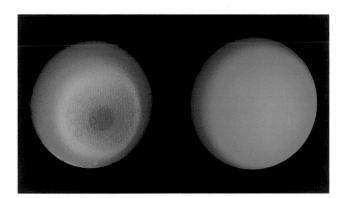

FALSE-COLOR VIEWS

Voyager 2's imaging system enabled it to take true and false-color views of Uranus. These highlighted the planet's atmospheric features and circulation patterns.

31

JOURNEY TO NEPTUNE

Voyager 2 sped past Neptune at 17 miles (27 km) per second on August 24, 1989. Radio signals from the spacecraft took 4 hours, 6 minutes to reach the Earth 2.78 billion miles (4.48 billion km) away. The signals arrived with the power equal to a fraction of one billionth of a watt. However, they contained an incredible mixture of data showing a blue planet with three main features: a Great Dark Spot, a wide band of clouds and white "scooter" clouds. The Great Dark Spot, which is the size of the Earth, circles around Neptune's equator every 18.3 hours, compared with the planet's own 19-hour rotation. The 2,680-mile (4,320-km)-wide band of clouds in the southern hemisphere has a Lesser Dark Spot. The "scooter" clouds travel at a speed of 400 miles (640 km) per hour.

Neptune was proving to be a more turbulent planet than its neighbor

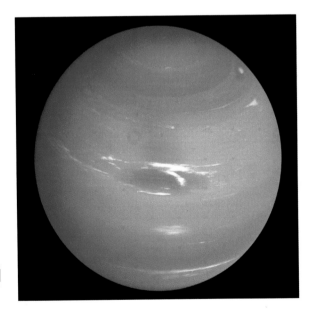

"SCOOTER" CLOUDS
The Great Dark Spot rotates counter-clockwise as it travels around Neptune. It is accompanied by white "scooter" clouds which are between 30 miles (50 km) and 60 miles (100 km) above the main atmosphere.

THE LESSER DARK SPOT

This view of Neptune's southern hemisphere shows the Lesser Dark Spot. It seems to "change lanes" during every circuit in the wide cloud bands.

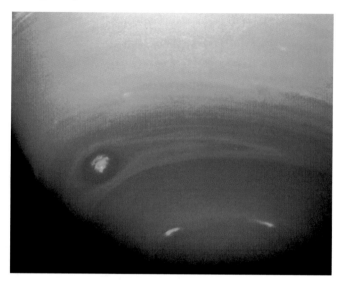

Uranus. The "scooter" clouds orbit mainly around the equator. They are like the cirrus clouds found on the Earth, but are made of methane ice. *Voyager 2* also found a ring system and four new moons, as well as imaging the remarkable world of Triton.

TRITON

Neptune's largest moon, Triton, is an extraordinary icy world of nitrogen and methane. Geysers on the moon's surface throw out liquid nitrogen 25 miles (40 km) up into space.

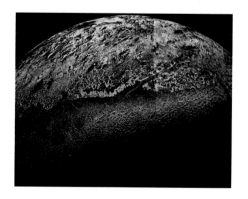

BEYOND OUR SYSTEM

 Four spacecrafts — *Pioneer 10* and *11* and *Voyager 1* and *2* — are heading out of the Solar System and deeper into the Universe. At the end of 1998, *Pioneer 10* was about 6.55 billion miles (10.55 billion km) from the Earth traveling at a speed of 7 miles (12 km) per second. It is heading for the star Aldebaran 68 light-years away. It will take *Pioneer 10* 2 million years to reach the star. Contact with *Pioneer 11* has been lost.

It is is heading toward the constellation Aquila and may pass one of its stars in 4 million years' time.

Voyager 1 is the most distant artificial object in space. It is 6.7 billion miles (10.8 billion km) from the Earth and heading toward an encounter with a dwarf star in the constellation Camelopardus in 400,000 years' time. *Voyager 2* is 5.2 billion (8.4 billion km) from the Earth, heading for a flyby of Sirius, the brightest star in the Earth's skies, in about 358,000 years' time. Engineers hope to keep communicating with *Voyager 2* until at least 2010.

THE PIONEER AGE
Pioneer 10, *which was launched in 1972 to visit Jupiter, is now heading toward the star Aldebaran in the constellation Taurus. The styles of the hair and clothing in this photograph show how much things have changed on Earth since the launch of* Pioneer 10 *almost 30 years ago.*

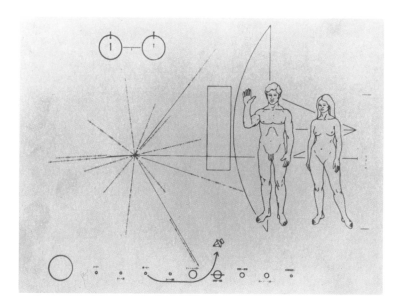

ON BOARD PIONEER

Pioneer 10 carries a plaque that depicts a man and a woman and indicates the position of the planet Earth in space — just in case intelligent beings ever find the spacecraft.

Each Pioneer spacecraft carries a gold-plated aluminum plaque measuring 6 by 9 inches (15 by 23 cm). The plaque is mounted on the spacecraft's antenna support struts, in a position that helps to shield it from erosion by interstellar dust. The plaque is etched with a diagram — it is a kind of picture message to any other intelligent beings that might exist in space. The diagram compares the height of the man and woman with that of the spacecraft. It also indicates the Earth's location in the Solar System in relation to the position of 14 pulsars.

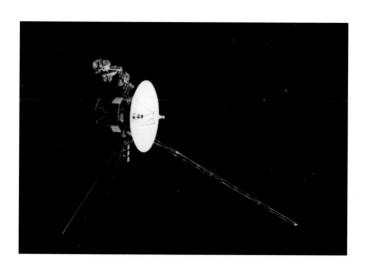

TO THE STARS

Voyager 1 is the most distant artificial object heading out of the Solar System. Traveling at a speed of 10.5 miles (17 km) per second, it is now heading toward the stars.

ROCKETS AND SATELLITES

Rocket technology made great advances following the end of World War II, based initially on Germany's V-2 guided missile. During the 1940s both the United States and the Soviet Union were launching research rockets, and by 1957 the Soviet Union was able to use a rocket to launch the first satellite into space. The first US satellite, *Explorer 1*, was launched the following year.

Today's generation of powerful rockets are used as launch vehicles

for a whole range of different probes and satellites. Satellites in orbit around the Earth make it possible for us to have instant telephone communications, receive TV pictures from the other side of the world, and exchange information via computer. Weather satellites monitor the world's weather, enabling forecasters to predict weather extremes such as hurricanes more accurately.

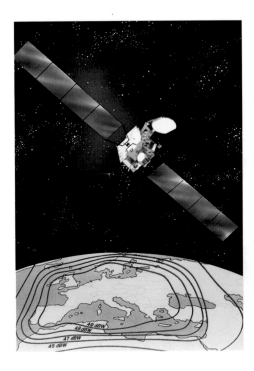

EARLY ROCKETS

Rockets that used a solid propellant such as gunpowder were launched by the Chinese as long ago as A.D.1200. However, the first liquid-propelled rocket was not launched until 1926, making the first major breakthrough in the development of space travel. The Soviet Union, the United States, and Germany began developing these rockets in the 1930s and the German *V-2* was put to deadly use in World War II. At the end of the war, many German rocket engineers went to the United States and the Soviet Union, helping these countries to make more powerful boosters. The *V-2* was modified to fly with the upper stage of a US Corporal rocket. The Viking, a highly successful US rocket became the basis for one of the first satellite launchers. The *V-2/Corporal*, nicknamed "Bumper", the *Viking* and *Aerobee* rockets, and many Soviet rockets were used to carry scientific instruments and animals into the lower reaches of space.

THE V-2 ROCKET
The V-2 rocket was developed by Germany during World War II. It fired over 3,000 missiles with deadly warheads. The rocket was later used by the USA to fly the first experiments into space.

UP AND DOWN

Another early space rocket was the Viking. Like the V-2, it flew an "up-and-down" flight, and not into orbit. It carried instruments that were later recovered after landing by parachute.

VIKING SERIES

The Viking high-altitude research rocket was launched 12 times, starting in 1949. One flight, *Viking 4*, was made from a ship. Its flight was typical of the missions flown by these booster rockets fueled by liquid oxygen and kerosene. *Viking 4* was used to measure atmospheric density, the speed of upper atmosphere winds, and cosmic-ray emissions, and to photograph the Earth from space. In 1954 *Viking 11* reached a record height of 156 miles (252 km).

AEROBEE ROCKET

This Aerobee rocket flew some of the first animals into space. The animals, such as mice, were recovered and examined to see how they had been affected by space travel.

LAUNCHERS

By 1957, developing rocket technology had enabled the first Earth satellite, *Sputnik 1*, to be launched. Since then, all kinds of spacecraft have continued to provide a valuable service to the Earth. Science satellites help us to learn more about how the Earth is affected by solar winds and radiation. A fleet of weather satellites provides continuous monitoring of the whole Earth. Communications satellites span the globe providing television, radio, and telephone communications all over the world. The Internet could not exist without satellites.

Navigation satellites guide ships and aircrafts and even help to control the operation of commercial trucking. Environmental satellites survey the world's resources. Military satellites, including spy satellites, help to keep the peace. Space satellites help to run this age of high technology.

EUROPE'S ARIANE
The Ariane 5 *rocket will help Europe to continue to lead the commercial market for launching satellites into geostationary and other Earth orbits.*

EARTH WATCH
Many different kinds of satellites are continually monitoring the Earth, providing data about its changing environment and resources.

THE SPACE BUSINESS

Space is big business, and governments are not the only organizations involved in it. Private companies build satellites and the launchers that put them into orbit. They also supply the infrastructure to allow services to be provided by the satellites. The cost of a typical communications satellite is $250 million. To launch it on a vehicle such as *Ariane 5* costs an extra $100 million. Further money is spent on insurance and the launch itself. So even before a satellite starts to work, it has cost about $500 million to put it in orbit.

MONITORING HURRICANES
Weather satellites provide a vital service by detecting the birth and development of hurricanes. These satellites plot the path of a hurricane so that early warnings can be given to people living in the affected areas.

41

SATELLITE TECHNOLOGY

Communications satellite technology has developed at a rapid rate. Just 30 years ago the rather basic Telstar satellite was transmitting TV signals to a ground station for onward transmission by land line to people's homes. Today, satellites can beam TV pictures directly into millions of homes — and from not just one channel but hundreds of different ones at the same time. Some important scientific advances have made this possible. First, we can now produce miniature components, such as traveling wave tube amplifiers. Also the satellites, with their perfectly

SIGNALS FROM SPACE
The antennas of communications satellites are "aimed" at specific user areas, called footprints. In these areas, highly amplified high-power signals are received by "dishes" that are as small as dinner plates.

fashioned antennas, have extremely high transmitting power — they are supplied with large amounts of electricity by advanced solar panels. Lastly, the high power transmissions

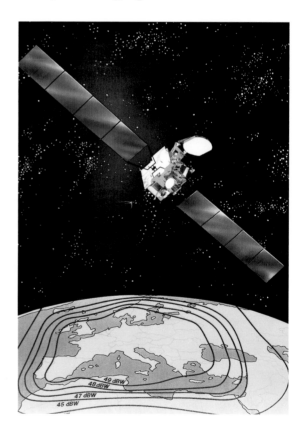

mean that satellite receiving dishes can be smaller. Satellites provide numerous communications services other than television. Some are able to handle 30,000 simultaneous phone, data, and fax calls.

SATELLITE SYSTEMS
The Iridium satellite system uses 66 operational satellites in a low orbit above the Earth. The satellites are positioned in such a way that a mobile phone user is within "line of sight" of at least one satellite at any time.

SATELLITE POWER

The 155-pound (77-kg) Telstar satellite, with solar cells providing 15 watts of electricity, used to transmit to a single receiving dish with a diameter of 82 feet (25 m). Today, a typical communications satellite weighs 7,700 pounds (3,500 kg) and has 30 amplifiers providing high power transmission in many wavebands. Using 6,000 watts of power from solar cells, it transmits to thousands of receiving dishes as small as 3 feet (90 cm) in diameter.

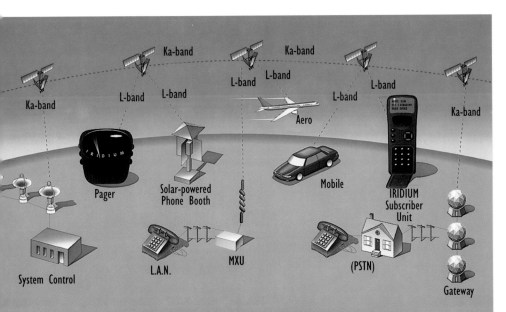

COMMUNICATING ON THE MOVE
Modern communications technology allows us to keep in touch with each other from almost anywhere in the world. The network of satellites in space provides instant communications whether by telephone, mobile phone, fax, pager, computer, or e-mail.

43

NAVIGATION SATELLITES

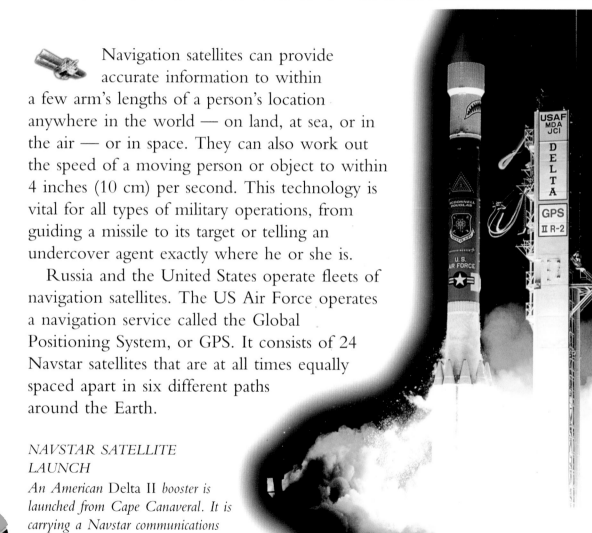

Navigation satellites can provide accurate information to within a few arm's lengths of a person's location anywhere in the world — on land, at sea, or in the air — or in space. They can also work out the speed of a moving person or object to within 4 inches (10 cm) per second. This technology is vital for all types of military operations, from guiding a missile to its target or telling an undercover agent exactly where he or she is.

Russia and the United States operate fleets of navigation satellites. The US Air Force operates a navigation service called the Global Positioning System, or GPS. It consists of 24 Navstar satellites that are at all times equally spaced apart in six different paths around the Earth.

NAVSTAR SATELLITE
LAUNCH
An American Delta II *booster is launched from Cape Canaveral. It is carrying a Navstar communications satellite into its circular 13,133-mile (21,182-km) orbit.*

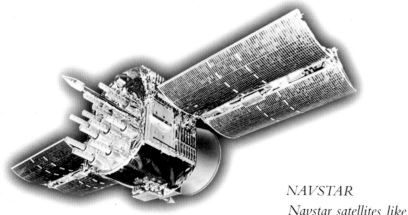

NAVSTAR
Navstar satellites like this one provide vital positioning information for all kinds of uses, from guiding a military fighter through the skies to helping lost sailors find their way at sea.

HOW GPS WORKS
Each GPS satellite continually transmits its position and the exact time of its transmission. A receiver on an aircraft or ship or carried by a hiker, for example, receives signals from four satellites at the same time. The receiver processes the data and displays the user's position and speed and the exact time. GPS has become a vital part of worldwide search and rescue. A search beacon on a liferaft in the middle of the ocean can be located and positioned accurately by GPS satellites.

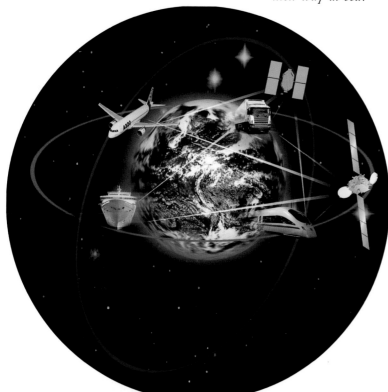

TRAFFIC CONTROL
Navigation technology that was originally developed for the military has now been transferred into the civilian sector. Soon even airlines will rely on satellites for air traffic control.

SPACE PROGRAMS

After the success of the first satellites in space, both the United States and Soviet Union embarked on their own space programs. The main part of each program consisted of a series of manned space flights. The Soviet Union's powerful rockets allowed them to launch large well-equipped spacecrafts able to sustain cosmonauts in space for several days. Meanwhile, the United States led the way with satellite technology

and also in the race to the Moon, which they eventually won.

The first flight of the Apollo Moon program took place in October 1968. In December 1968, the three astronauts on board *Apollo 8* orbited the Moon 10 times. By July of the following year, the first person had set foot on the surface of the Moon. American astronauts made five further landings on the Moon between 1969 and 1972.

RACE TO THE MOON

 In 1961 President John F. Kennedy decided to respond to the Soviet "threat" of dominance in space. He announced to the US Congress on May 25, that he wanted his country to land men on the Moon before 1970. The space project would cost more than $25

billion and would require a series of manned space flights to prove the technology, and Moon scouts to check out the new territory. What became known as Project Apollo was one of the most extraordinary undertakings of the twentieth century. It was undertaken on the assumption that the Soviet Union was also planning to send men to the Moon, so the "space race" became known as the "Moon race."

Space flight dominated the 1960s, hardly ever leaving the front pages of newspapers as important steps in the Apollo project were taken year by year. These events led up to the momentous first manned landing on the Moon in July 1969.

FIRST AMERICAN IN SPACE
Twenty-three days after Soviet cosmonaut Yuri Gagarin became the first person in space, Alan Shepard became the first American in space in the Mercury capsule Freedom 7.

SHEPARD'S SPLASHDOWN
US astronaut Alan Shepard is hauled aboard a helicopter after completing his 15 minute up-and-down space flight with a planned splashdown in the Atlantic Ocean.

MAN ON THE MOON
President Kennedy's goal was to place an American on the Moon by 1969. When he announced the Moon project, the USA had just 15 minutes of manned space flight experience.

49

FIRST APOLLO FLIGHTS

After the three-man crew of *Apollo 7* successfully tested the command and service modules in Earth orbit, a decision was made to send *Apollo 8* to the Moon. The Unite States feared that the Soviet Union was about to send two cosmonauts around the Moon on a fly-by mission. So the planned *Apollo 8* lunar module test flight in Earth orbit was canceled. Instead, *Apollo 8* was sent to make 10 orbits of the Moon. The mission was one of the biggest milestones in space history and one of the major events of the twentieth century.

The three astronauts in *Apollo 8* were launched on December 21, 1968. While orbiting the Moon over Christmas they sent back messages

LAUNCH OF APOLLO 7
A smaller Saturn 1B *rocket boosts* Apollo 7 *into orbit on the first manned flight of the Apollo space program. The three-man crew made a successful 11-day flight, proving the command and service module systems.*

of goodwill and read from the Bible.
Apollo 8 came to within 66 miles (110 km) of the Moon's surface. The memorable flight ended with a safe splashdown in the Pacific Ocean — and the astronauts brought back the first photo of the rising Earth as seen from the Moon.

MOON CRATER
The first close look at the Moon was made during the Apollo 8 *mission. This is the crater Langrenus taken by* Apollo 8*'s photographer, Bill Anders, while orbiting the Moon.*

CREW OF APOLLO 8
The first men to fly to the Moon were Frank Borman, James Lovell, and Bill Anders. They made 10 orbits of the Moon in their Apollo 8 *spacecraft during Christmas 1968.*

MAN ON THE MOON

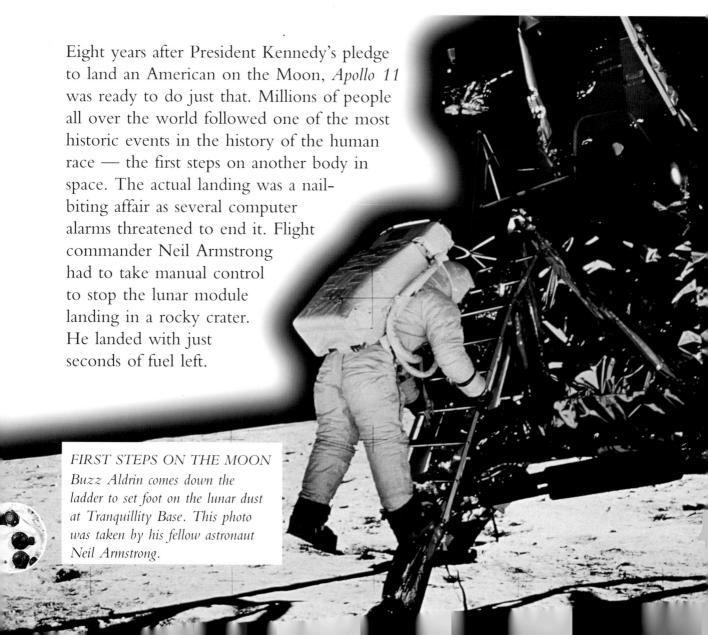

Eight years after President Kennedy's pledge to land an American on the Moon, *Apollo 11* was ready to do just that. Millions of people all over the world followed one of the most historic events in the history of the human race — the first steps on another body in space. The actual landing was a nail-biting affair as several computer alarms threatened to end it. Flight commander Neil Armstrong had to take manual control to stop the lunar module landing in a rocky crater. He landed with just seconds of fuel left.

FIRST STEPS ON THE MOON
Buzz Aldrin comes down the ladder to set foot on the lunar dust at Tranquillity Base. This photo was taken by his fellow astronaut Neil Armstrong.

Thanks to satellite technology, millions were able to follow events live on TV. The high point was watching the first walk on the Moon, as Armstrong's ghostly looking figure stepped off the footpad of the lunar module *Eagle*. He was followed by Buzz Aldrin, and both set to work deploying two science instruments and collecting samples of rock to bring back to Earth. The third *Apollo 11* astronaut, Mike Collins, stayed on board the command module.

APOLLO 11'S CREW
Neil Armstrong (left), Michael Collins (center) and Buzz Aldrin (right) pose for a formal crew portrait a few weeks before the launch of their epic Apollo 11 *mission to the Moon.*

MOON MISQUOTES

No one knew what Neil Armstrong was going to say when he placed his right boot onto the lunar surface. He only decided finally after he had landed safely. He said that he didn't see the point in worrying about what to say when he didn't know whether he would land successfully — he believed that they had a 50-50 chance of success. Unfortunately, Armstrong's remark became one of the most misquoted in history. He meant to say, "That's one small step for a man, one giant leap for mankind." He actually said, "That's one small step for man, one giant leap for mankind."

SHUTTLES AND STATIONS

When the first Space Shuttle took off in 1981, it marked a major milestone in the history of space exploration. With its ability to land back on Earth like an airplane, the Shuttle is the first manned spacecraft that can be reused. It has made an important contribution to satellite technology. Shuttle astronauts not only deploy communications and other satellites in space, but they even retrieve and repair damaged ones while remaining in space. The Hubble Space

Telescope, which has sent back so
many spectacular images of space,
was deployed by the Shuttle.

The Space Shuttle has also
ferried astronauts to the *Mir* space
station, launched by the Soviet
Union in 1986. Extra modules have
been added to extend the station. *Mir*
has received astronauts and scientists
from many different countries. The first
parts of a new international space station
were assembled in space in 1998.

THE SPACE SHUTTLE

The Space Shuttle consists of three main parts: the orbiter spaceplane, two solid rocket boosters, and an external propellant tank. The shuttle is launched using three main engines attached to the orbiter. The engines are fed with propellants from the external tank (ET) and by two solid propellant strap-on solid rocket boosters (SRB). The SRBs use up their fuel after 2 minutes and are ejected. They are recovered for reuse in later flights. The orbiter and its ET continue flying for 6 more minutes until the initial orbit is reached. The ET is then jettisoned. The orbiter's orbital maneuvering system (OMS) engines and reaction control system (RCS) thrusters are used to change the orbit and perform maneuvers.

At the end of the flight, the OMS engines are fired and the orbiter plunges into the Earth's atmosphere at 25 times the speed of sound. The friction causes its 34,000 heat shield tiles to heat up to 2,880 degrees Fahrenheit (1,600 degrees Celsius). The orbiter then lands like a glider.

orbiter

external tank

solid rocket booster

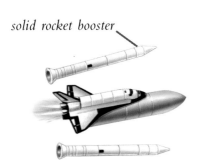

SHUTTLE LAUNCH
Two minutes after the Shuttle takes off, the solid rocket boosters are ejected and fall back to Earth by parachute. Six minutes later, the external tank is jettisoned and is destroyed as it reenters the Earth's atmosphere.

56

ASSEMBLING THE SHUTTLE
The Space Shuttle is assembled vertically inside the Vehicle Assembly Building at the Kennedy Space Center. It is rolled out to the launch pad on a mobile launch platform.

"FLYING BRICK"
The orbiter makes a carefully controlled approach to its landing site. It descends at an angle seven times steeper than that of a normal airliner, with a nose-down angle of 28 degrees. The vehicle finally lands at a speed of more than 200 miles per hour (300 km/h).
The Shuttle has been nicknamed by astronauts as the "flying brick". The commander and pilot of Shuttle missions make hundreds of practice landings using a specially adapted training aircraft.

LANDING OPERATIONS
Immediately after landing, the orbiter is surrounded by a crowd of vehicles and engineers. They prepare it for transfer to the Shuttle Processing Facility where the orbiter is made ready for its next flight.

SKYLAB

 Launched in 1973, *Skylab* was America's first and so far only space station — until the launch of the first American section of the International Space Station 25 years later. Much of *Skylab* was made of equipment developed for the Apollo program. Its main orbital workshop comprised a fully equipped

empty upper stage of a *Saturn V* rocket. The Apollo telescope mount was based on a leftover lunar module. *Skylab* was launched using a *Saturn V* rocket, and crews were sent to the space station aboard Apollo command service modules that docked with the space station.

Three crews were launched to *Skylab*, consisting of several astronauts who would have flown later Apollo missions that had been canceled. Each crew included one scientist astronaut. The first crew had to repair the space station after it was damaged during launch. The final crew stayed in the space station for 84 days.

SKYLAB *DAMAGE*
Skylab was damaged during launch and lost one of its solar panels. Another panel was successfully deployed during a brave space walk, saving the whole Skylab program.

FLOATING AROUND
Scientist astronaut Edward Gibson floats into the orbital workshop during the third and last Skylab *mission in 1973 and 1974. It lasted 84 days, which was an American record.*

DANGEROUS WORK

In May, 1973 former *Apollo 12* astronaut Pete Conrad and scientist Doctor Joe Kerwin performed the bravest and most dangerous space walk in history soon after reaching *Skylab.* They had to prise out the space station's remaining solar array, which was vital to producing power. The other array had been torn off during launch. Conrad and Kerwin used wire cutters to free the jammed panel and pulled it out using pullies that they rigged during the space walk. When it was freed, the panel sprang out and almost hit the space-walking duo.

SCIENTIFIC STUDY
Skylab *was a fully equipped science base, with one section devoted to astronomy and the study of the Sun. Here, scientist Gibson mans the operating console for the telescope.*

THE MIR SPACE STATION

 The *Mir* space station is Russia's extraordinary success story. It was still operating in 1999 13 years after the launch of its first module. The space station consists of the *Mir* core module and a small *Kvant 1* module attached to its rear. Soyuz manned spacecraft and Progress unmanned tankers can dock at a port on the *Kvant 1* module. Attached to the front of the core module is a docking module with five ports. One is used for Soyuz ferries and the other four are for modules that were launched later. The whole space station, with six modules, a Progress tanker and a Soyuz spacecraft, weighs about 130 tons.

WORKING TOGETHER
Russian cosmonaut Yuri Gidzenko and German astronaut Thomas Reiter at work on board the Mir *space station in 1996. The two men also went on space walks together.*

MIR *OVER NEW ZEALAND*
*The first part of the Mir space
station was launched in February
1986, and the final module was
added in 1996. The core station
was based on earlier Salyut modules.
Mir is pictured here orbiting over
Cape Farewell, on the northern
tip of South Island, New Zealand.*

FOREIGN ASTRONAUTS

Thomas Reiter, a German astronaut representing the European Space Agency, flew a 179-day mission on *Mir*. Six American astronauts, including Shannon Lucid and Michael Foale, have also stayed on *Mir* for more than 100 days. France has also flown commercial missions on the space station. One of the French astronauts was Jean Loup Chretien who also flew on *Salyut 7* — and revisited *Mir* in a Space Shuttle! Shorter missions have been flown by other countries, including Afghanistan and Syria.

Mir has hosted almost 30 main crews, including one cosmonaut who stayed on board for a record 437 days. In addition, many visiting crews have included astronauts from other countries, including the United States, the UK and Germany. Foreign countries have paid Russia for the scientific experiment time on board and for the space flight experience.

INDEX

A
Aldrin, Buzz 52, 53
Apollo missions 47, 48-49,
    50-51
  Skylab 58, 59
  spacecraft 18-19, 52-53
Aquila constellation 34
Ariane rockets 40, 41,
Armstrong, Neil 52,
    53
asteroids exploration
    9, 10
atmosphere
  Earth 12, 56
  Jupiter 10, 26, 27
  Mars 39
  Sun 12
  Titan 28, 29
  Uranus 30, 31
  Venus 16

B
Borman, Frank 19, 51

C
Cape Canaveral 44
Cassini-Huygens spacecraft 10,
    11
Cassini orbiter 28, 29
comets exploration 9, 10

communications satellites 37,
    40, 41, 42-43

D
Delta II rocket 37, 44

E
Earth in space 18-19, 35
European Space Agency 11,
    61
Explorer satellites 36

F
Foale, Michael 61
Freedom spacecraft 48

G
Gagarin, Yuri 48
Galileo spacecraft 24, 26, 27
Gemini spacecraft 47
gravity 13
  Jupiter 24
  Saturn 29
  Venus 14

H
Hubble Space telescope space
    shuttle 54-55
Huygens probe 11, 28, 29

I
International Space Station 58

J
Jupiter 9
  exploration 24-27
  spacecraft 10, 26, 28,34

K
Kennedy Space Centre 57

L
launch vehicles 36, 40-41
life
  Mars 22
Lovell, James 18, 19, 51

M
Mariner probes 10, 14-17, 22
Mars
  asteroids 9
  exploration 10, 11, 22-23
Mercury
  exploration 14-15
meteorites 14
Mir space station 54, 55,
    60-61
Miranda 30, 31
Moon
  Apollo missions 50-51

landing 8, 10, 52-53
probes 12, 20-21
race 48-49
space programs 47
view of Earth 18
moons
Jupiter 26
Saturn 28, 29
Uranus 30, 31

N
NASA 11, 37
Neptune
exploration 30, 32-33

O
Oberon 31
orbits 13

P
Pathfinder spacecraft 22, 23
Pioneer spacecraft 9, 12, 24, 28, 34-35
planets
exploration 8, 9,10
Pluto
exploration 8, 10

R
rockets 36-37, 38-39

S
Salyut spacecraft 61
satellites 8, 36-37, 42-43
first 36
navigation 40, 44-45
scientific 40
weather 36, 37, 40, 41
Saturn
exploration 10, 11, 24, 28-29
Saturn rockets 50, 58
Shepard, Alan 47, 48, 49
Sirius (star) 34
Skylab 12, 55, 58-59
SOHO 9, 12, 13
Sojourner rover 22, 23
Solar System
exploration 8, 10, 17, 34, 35
Soyuz spacecraft
Mir 60
space shuttle 54-55, 56-57
launches 17, 26
space stations 61
space stations 54-55
Skylab 12, 58
Sputnik satellites 8, 40
Sun exploration 10, 12-13
Surveyor spacecraft 8, 20, 21

T
Taurus constellation 34
telescopes
Skylab 59
solar 12
Telstar satellite 42, 43
TIROS 1 36
Titan (moon) 10, 11, 28, 29
Titan rockets 11, 47

U
ultraviolet rays
observation 13
Universe
exploration 34-35
Uranus 33
exploration 30-31

V
Venera probes 16, 17
Venus 9
exploration 10, 14, 15, 16-17
Viking spacecraft 22, 23, 37, 38, 39
Viking 1 8, 11
Voyager spacecraft 28, 29, 32, 33
Voyager 1 24, 28, 34, 35
Voyager 2 24, 30, 31, 34

ACKNOWLEDGMENTS

The publishers wish to thank the following artists who have
contributed to this book.

Julian Baker, Kuo Kang Chen, Rob Jakeway, Darrell Warner
(Beehive Illustrations) Guy Smith, Janos Marffy,
Peter Sarson.

Photographs supplied by Genesis Photo Library and
Miles Kelly Archive.